Natural Turns

Freeskiing and Other
EXTREME SNOW SPORTS

Elliott Smith

raintree 🍃

a Capstone company — publishers for children

Raintree is an imprint of Capstone Global Library Limited, a company incorporated in England and Wales having its registered office at 264 Banbury Road, Oxford, OX2 7DY – Registered company number: 6695582

www.raintree.co.uk
myorders@raintree.co.uk

Text © Capstone Global Library Limited 2021
The moral rights of the proprietor have been asserted.

Edited by Anna Butzer
Designed by Cynthia Della-Rovere
Media research by Kelly Garvin
Original illustrations © Capstone Global Library Limited 2020
Production by Katy LaVigne
Originated by Capstone Global Library Ltd
Printed and bound in India

978 1 4747 9362 9 (hardback)
978 1 4747 9681 1 (paperback)

Acknowledgements
We would like to thank the following for permission to reproduce photographs: Associated Press/Christian Pondella/Red Bull Content Pool via AP Images, 4-5; Newscom/Andrew Wilz/Icon SMI, 25; Shutterstock: Alexander Rochau, cover, backcover, alexfe, 9, Budimir Jevtic, 28, Dmytro Vietrov, 12, gorillaimages, 27, Ipatov, 11, Leopoldo Lunghi, 21, McKerrell Photography, 23, Parilov, 17, 19, Savostin Ivan, 6, yanik88, 15. Artistic elements: Shutterstock: Edu Silva 2ev, nattanan726, pupsy

Every effort has been made to contact copyright holders of material reproduced in this book. Any omissions will be rectified in subsequent printings if notice is given to the publisher.

All the internet addresses (URLs) given in this book were valid at the time of going to press. However, due to the dynamic nature of the internet, some addresses may have changed, or sites may have changed or ceased to exist since publication. While the author and publisher regret any inconvenience this may cause readers, no responsibility for any such changes can be accepted by either the author or the publisher.

Contents

CHAPTER 1

A world of powder

Standing at the top of a snow-covered mountain, the sound of silence is loud. The route to the bottom is straight down. But at the **apex** of some of the world's biggest peaks, freeskier Michelle Parker isn't scared. Instead, she's happy. Whether she is in the mountains of Alaska or Europe, the path she creates is her own.

Michelle Parker skis in the mountains near Mammoth Lakes, California, in the United States.

"The freedom of choosing my own way down the mountain had me hooked," Parker said about freeskiing.

One of Parker's most memorable skis happened in Japan. Myoko Kogen is one of the country's oldest ski resorts. Some skiers say it is home to the best snow in the world. Parker helped create a skiing film about the area, highlighting the natural beauty and tree-lined runs. She said that being in the outdoors and flying down the mountain is a unique feeling. "When you feel that when you're skiing, it does make it more of a special experience," she said.

CHAPTER 2

What is freeskiing?

There's only one way down from the top of a mountain. Or is there? Freeskiing athletes are able to explore the natural **terrain** during their runs. There are no rules, no set paths and no **gates** to follow.

Many freeskiing athletes enjoy the sport because they are able to ski freely, anywhere and on any terrain they want to ski on.

Usually, freeskiing features big, fast turns and long, steep **vertical descents**. It also features cliff drops. Freeskiing gives athletes the chance to create their own course. They can create unique **lines**, attempt jumps or build tricks, all while flying down the slope. Freeskiing is sometimes called big mountain skiing to help separate it from freestyle skiing.

Freestyle skiing competitions are usually timed races. Skiers try to get the best time on the course. Freeskiing doesn't have a time element. It's more focused on creativity and difficulty. Freeskiing athletes enjoy the thrill of the ride. Skiers try to find less popular mountains to freeski down.

terrain physical features of a place
gates narrow poles with flags attached; some skiers carve around gates
vertical straight up and down
descent downward slope
line path down a mountain or hill

When it comes to freeski mountains, bigger is better. Many big mountain courses are not available to **recreational** skiers because of the danger involved. Some of the best places for freeskiing are in the United States. They include Crested Butte in Colorado and Big Sky Resort in Montana. Big Sky's course has a 1,326-metre vertical drop!

Skiing at the 2022 Olympics

Although freeskiing is not an Olympic sport, there will be lots of skiing events to watch during the next Olympic Games. The freestyle events in Beijing will feature five events: moguls, halfpipe, ski cross, aerials and ski slopestyle. All of these events include big jumps, cool tricks and high speeds. Some events are judged, while others are races. Though the courses sometimes use dry snow, watching them will still give you a rush.

recreational activity pursued for enjoyment
stable not easily moved

A freeskiing athlete hits the slopes
at Big Sky Resort in Montana, USA.

The skis used on big mountains are different from traditional skis. Most freeskis are longer and heavier than traditional skis. Athletes need to be **stable** when going fast on rough snow and steep terrain. Most freeskiers use skis that are taller than they are because the length helps with stability.

Visual glossary

goggles
Goggles protect an athlete's eyes from all winter elements, including wind and the glare of the sun reflecting off snow.

poles
Many athletes use poles to help with rhythm and balance, especially on steep slopes.

salopettes (snow trousers)
Salopettes should be waterproof and flexible enough for an athlete to move freely.

boots
Boots should fit snugly with one pair of socks. This combination will keep feet warm and dry.

helmet
Stay safe when hitting the slopes!
A helmet can prevent head injury.

jacket
A jacket is the outer layer
of clothing an athlete
wears. It protects from
the snow and harsh wind.

gloves
Gloves keep an athlete's
hands warm in harsh
conditions. They
should be flexible and
waterproof. Some
athletes bring an extra
pair of gloves, in case
the first pair gets wet.

bindings
Bindings should be
adjusted to fit boots.

skis
The proper ski length varies for
each athlete. The usual length is
somewhere between the top of
an athlete's head and their chin.

11

CHAPTER 3

Snowboarding

A combination of surfing, skateboarding and skiing, snowboarding has boomed in popularity in recent years. The sport's origins date back to the 1960s with the invention of the "Snurfer", a sledge-like board. The board allowed riders to surf on snow. Other creators began making improvements, eventually leading to attaching ski boots to the board.

Snowboards today are high-tech creations that give athletes the ability to perform crazy tricks and tackle steep mountains. While most people can try snowboarding, only the most extreme athletes will have a go at big mountain snowboarding. After all, going down a cliff called The Shoulder of Death is a little bit scary!

What makes big mountain snowboarding so difficult is a combination of speed and control. Without ski poles to help control the body, these athletes must be masters at **manoeuvring** the board. Many of the best snowboarders say their board becomes almost a part of themselves as they rocket down mountains.

A snowboarder performs a trick called a lein, where their front hand grabs the heel edge of their board.

While most big mountain riders participate for fun, there are competitions for the top athletes. These events are judged based on rider lines, jumps and board control.

Tricks are a huge part of snowboarding. The Elbow Curve is a move during which a rider places one arm on the ground and spins the board. When doing a Backside 180, a rider almost completes a full rotation and then does a reverse spin at the end.

manoeuvre make planned and controlled movements that require skill

CHAPTER 4

Snowkiting

Most people think about kites at the beach, but in snowkiting, the fun comes to the mountains. Similar to windsurfing, snowkiting uses the power of a breeze to help create an extreme ride. The sport began in Europe in the 1970s and has spread across the globe.

Athletes use large foil kites that are controlled by either two or four lines. These kites are a bit like a parachute. Because the kites are soft, there is no damage when they fall to the ground. They can easily be relaunched after a crash and packed away at the end of the day. Athletes pair a kite with skis or a snowboard, depending on what they **prefer**. Larger kites are harder to control but provide more power, which is why experts use them.

prefer like one thing more than another

While snowkiting can take place anywhere there's snow and wind, advanced athletes can bring their equipment to the mountains. There, the wind allows them to go both up, down and even sideways along the slope. Depending on the wind and terrain, snowkiters can soar in the air as the kite pulls them upwards. Because snow is usually quite a smooth surface, you don't need a lot of wind for a successful flight.

Snowkiting can be done on mountains or big hills, but flat ground is ideal.

The world's most difficult snowkiting race, Ragnarok, is a 129-kilometre (80-mile), five-lap marathon. Only a few of the racers finish in the five-hour time frame. Racers must dodge other kites, **slalom** through rocks and battle difficult wind conditions to succeed.

slalom downhill race in which riders weave through sets of poles

CHAPTER 5

Ski cycling

Another combination of two sports, ski cycling gives riders a unique way to travel down the slopes. On the surface, the idea seems simple. Remove the wheels from a bike frame and attach a pair of skis. When riders are ready, they attach a pair of short skis to their feet and hit the trail! Ski cycling is sometimes called skibobbing to help differentiate it from normal cycling. The first ski bikes date back to the 1800s, where they helped **transport** goods through mountains.

transport move or carry something or someone from one place to another

Ski cycling can be much easier to pick up than skiing. If riding a bike comes naturally, this might be a good way to start doing some activity on the mountain. And unlike skiing, ski cycling is gentle on a skier's knees. Some big mountain areas are making room for ski bikes as the sport continues to grow.

Ski cycling is growing in popularity around the globe.

Ski bikes can be expensive to purchase, but some resorts offer rental bikes that can be used. In addition, there are kits that upgrade old bikes into ski bikes for a fraction of the price.

Professional ski bikers take part in races, located mostly in Europe. The speed record on a ski bike is 201 km per hour (125 miles per hour), set during a race in France in 2003.

Fat tyre biking

Fat tyre cycling is another way to get rolling on the snow. Riders who used their mountain bikes to explore trails in the summer wanted to use their bikes all year round. So, they came up with a unique solution. Athletes replaced the bike's normal tyres with oversized tyres that gave maximum **traction**. The tyres are usually between 10 and 12.7 centimetres wide. This gives riders the ability to pedal through the snow and uphill without slipping. The Fat Bike World Championships is a 40-km (25-mile) cross-country race held in Colorado, USA, where riders tackle all types of terrain.

Fat tyre bikes allow cycling enthusiasts to cycle no matter what the weather conditions.

traction amount of grip one surface has while moving over another surface

CHAPTER 6

Snocross

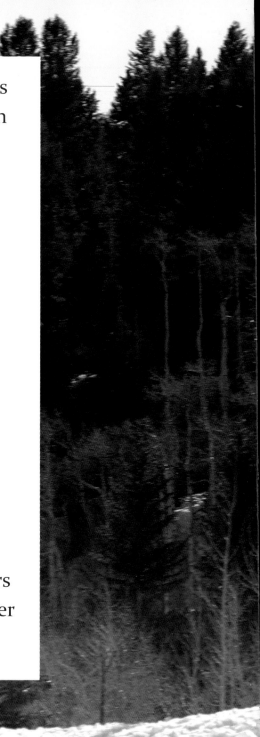

The high-speed sport of snocross brings the power of engines to fresh powder for thrilling competitions. Snocross features snowmobiles zooming through natural courses, where athletes must pull off jumps and make tight turns. The sport developed from motocross, which shares many of the same characteristics as the snow event.

The machines used in snocross, usually called sledges, are very powerful. The weight of an average sledge is 210 kilograms. They can reach heights of up to 30 metres when jumping off ramps.

Snocross races are intense. Riders battle for position while soaring over jumps and other **obstacles**.

Professional snocross athletes race at speeds up to 97 km per hour (60 miles per hour).

Snocross is gaining popularity across the world. Events such as the X Games and the Snocross Series Tour draw big crowds. Snocross athletes have played a role in this growth by hosting youth clinics. These events give young riders an opportunity to learn how to improve both on and off the track.

obstacle object or barrier that competitors must avoid during a race

CHAPTER 7

Where to begin

Michelle Parker is one of the few women who participates in big mountain freeskiing. She wants to help create awareness of the sport and get more girls and women involved. That's why she makes films of her adventures down some of the world's toughest mountains.

"The next generation of women needs strong role models, and I want to be that," says Parker.

Skiing and other snow sports are a great way to experience winter fun. However, it is important for beginners to make safety and training a priority before hitting the slopes.

The first step is to have all the proper equipment, and to ensure that it is the right size and fit. Beginner skis and snowboards should be short and flexible. This makes them easier to turn and control. Boots should be flexible so knees can go over the toes. All bindings should be checked by a ski technician. A helmet that fits properly is a must. Winter sports athletes should always dress warmly.

Beginners should practise stopping safely and controlling their speed at all times.

Many ski resorts and snowboard parks have **certified** instructors who can help teach beginners the important first steps. Learning from a pro can make the process easier and more fun. Practising on the bunny slope or smallest ramp can help solidify the right moves. Always practise with a parent or instructor nearby. As a bonus, many resorts offer free lessons to beginner skiers.

The elite athletes in extreme freeskiing and snowboarding have been on the slopes since they were very young. It takes years of practice and training to attempt any extreme ski, jump or race. Snow sport participants should always be aware of potential dangers. Some dangers include weather, obstacles and other skiers or boarders. Being careful on the slopes helps to keep everyone safer.

Getting out in the snow is a great way to appreciate natural beauty. Pick a snow sport, keep practising and get ready to have some *great* adventures!

Being safe on the slopes includes wearing bright colours that can be easily seen by other athletes.

certified having officially recognized training, skills and abilities

GLOSSARY

apex highest point of something

certified having officially recognized training, skills and abilities

descent downward slope

gates narrow poles with flags attached; some skiers carve around gates

line path down a mountain or hill

manoeuvre make planned and controlled movements that require skill

obstacle object or barrier that competitors must avoid during a race

prefer like one thing more than another

recreational activity pursued for enjoyment

slalom downhill race in which riders weave through sets of poles

stable not easily moved

terrain physical features of a place

traction amount of grip one surface has while moving over another surface

transport move or carry something or someone from one place to another

vertical straight up and down

FIND OUT MORE

BOOKS

Extreme Snow and Ice Sports (Sports to the Extreme),
Erin K. Butler (Raintree, 2017)

Half-Pipe Panic (Sport Stories Graphic Novels),
Brendon Terrell (Raintree, 2019)

WEBSITES

www.bbc.co.uk/sport/get-inspired/25912976
Top tips about how to get into (and best enjoy) snowsports.

dkfindout.com/uk/sports/snowboarding
Discover more snowboarding facts and statistics, including an
interactive visual glossary.

INDEX